VIEWS OF MACKINAC ISLAND

Views of

MACKINAC ISLAND

THOMAS KACHADURIAN

Sleeping Bear Press

Sleeping Bear Press
310 North Main Street
P.O. Box 20
Chelsea, MI 48118
www.sleepingbearpress.com

Printed and bound in Canada.

10 9 8 7 6 5 4 3 2 1

Library of Congress Cataloging-in-Publication Data

Kachadurian, Thomas.
Views of Mackinac Island / Thomas Kachadurian.
p. cm.
ISBN 1-58536-006-6
1. Mackinac Island (Mich. : Island)—Pictorial works. 2. Mackinac
Island (Mich. : Island)—Description and travel. 3. Mackinac Island
(Mich. : Island)—History. I. Title.
F572.M16 K13 2000
977.4'923—dc21
00-010313

Perhaps more than anywhere in the world,
no man is an island on Mackinac.
This book would not have been possible without friends.
I have enjoyed the assistance and advice of David Armour,
Brad Chambers, Dan Crow, Brian Dunnigan, Jeff Dykehouse,
Lorabeth and John Fitzgerald, Robert Jerstrom, Larry and Nancy
Keogh, Trish Martin, Karen McCarthy, Carl Nold, Phil Porter,
Lornie Porter, Jay Stingel, Tim Tanner, and Colleen Zelt.

For technical advice, historical resources, cultural translation
and reality checks I am indebted to Carolyn Artman.

Julie, Madeline, and Noah—I'll be home for dinner.

TABLE OF CONTENTS

Mackinac Island is a Victorian woman with expensive tastes. She is lovely to look at and every minute you spend with her is filled with delight. But ultimately, all of your efforts at courtship will never lead to engagement, and marriage is just plain out of the question. She is not spoken for, but has been held by so many others who have tried to make her their own that she has grown weary of possessiveness. Those who enjoy her company most are those who treasure each day's passing, knowing full well they will someday depart, hoping only to be allowed, at some point, to return.

Several family names have become synonymous with contemporary Mackinac Island: Brown and Sheppler, Chambers and Musser, Harry Ryba. They merely join a list of other suitors—Astor and Biddle, Beaumont and Marquette, Madame LaFramboise—who have left their gifts for the fair maiden. She carries their memory with her always, but, as independence is her way, she will always move on.

Only the 700 or so permanent residents of Mackinac Island ever see our lady without her make-up, but they are her handmaidens and sworn to secrecy. They see her moody and brooding side in November when the wind is cold and the mud begins to harden, and in March when the tourists have long since left and the ice refuses to melt. They

ABOVE RIGHT: *Today's Harbor View Inn was once the home of Madame LaFramboise, a dynamic nineteenth century Mackinac Island woman who successfully navigated the male dominated fur trade when she took control of her husband's business after he was murdered .*

have learned not to squander their fortunes on her whims, but are willing also to stay with her despite her very nature, which creates everyday challenges. She forces them to ride snowmobiles miles across the frozen lake just for groceries. Late in winter, when the ice is weak, and before the first boats cross, even her grace and charm become tedious; the only brief escape is sneaking to the airport behind her back and paying dearly for a flight out.

Only those who die by her side remain with her, and they rest near her heart. Where they sleep, deep in the woods, they are protected from the winter winds and are bothered only a bit by the din of summer. In the end, no man or woman can own Mackinac Island. Only she can hold them.

Round Island, view from West Bluff.

Limestone boulders along the west shore lead to limestone cliffs above.

There is little consensus about the *Origins of Mackinac* Island. In one version of a Chippewa legend, there was a three-day fog over their fishing ground, and when the fog lifted, Mackinac Island was there, trees full-grown, flowers in bloom. In another legend—the native equivalent of the Judeo-Christian Great Flood—the whole earth was covered with water. The great hare, *Michibou*, created Mackinac Island by blowing on a single grain of sand he retrieved from bottom of Lake Huron. From this, Mackinac's first people believed, all life grew.

It could well be that the Christian missionaries, who recorded the native legends, applied their own Great Flood analogies to the story. It could also be that early Chippewa, Huron, and Ottawa were paddling around looking for a place to land just about the same time that Noah was getting tired of the smell, thinking about how one of those two sheep might taste on the barbeque. Even scientists agree that there was once lots of water over the land that we Michiganders now call home.

Whether the land came up, or the water went down, there is agreement that Mackinac Island was carved by nature's hand. She started her work more than 350 million years ago, carving and cementing limestone stacks with groundwater. As the water receded, softer materials were washed away leaving the stone structures towering above the land.

About 11,000 years ago, as the glaciers receded, most of Michigan was underwater in what geologists call the Main Algonquin Stage. Lakes Huron and Michigan were one big pond

The most-likely-to-appear-on-a-postcard limestone formation, Arch Rock.

and only the smallest part of Mackinac Island, the area near Lookout Point and Fort Holmes, was above the water, with Sugarloaf growing out of the lake near the ancient Island's northeast shore. Native Americans believed Sugarloaf, the Island's most noticeable limestone stack, to be either the wigwam of the great spirit *Gitchi Manitou*, or the home of his man-messenger, *Manibozho*. It is possible that these legends date back to a time when Sugarloaf stretched up from the surface of Lake Algonquin, and appeared to be subordinate to, not part of, Mackinac Island.

Today limestone defines Mackinac Island. Fort Mackinac is built on a limestone cliff, its walls fashioned from cracked stone cemented with resins made from limestone powder. Grand Hotel looks out from a prehistoric limestone ridge. In Michigan, a state so characterized by sand, the limestone on Mackinac Island is striking. Many of the Island's legendary features are carved from limestone. Skull Cave, Arch Rock, and Devil's Kitchen are the usual suspects. But even the clearing around Anne's Tablet is framed by a limestone shell that makes it uniquely Mackinac Island.

ABOVE AND RIGHT: *Sugarloaf.*

It is difficult to mark *The Beginning of Tourism* to Mackinac Island. Native people came here seasonally long before anyone recorded history. But they were here on business, primarily fishing, and for spiritual renewal. There is also evidence that seventeenth and eighteenth century fur traders and voyageurs enjoyed the Island's natural beauty, but it was still nothing more than a truck stop on the Great Lakes highway. By the middle of the nineteenth century fishing again ruled, but it was smelly business, and Mackinac was better suited to sweeter occupations.

Nineteenth century intellectuals discovered Nature, not as wilderness to be endured, but as the mark of a higher power to be celebrated. These "rugged individualists" sought Mackinac Island for adventure. They were the first to come to the Island to spend money rather than to make it. They knew a good thing when they saw it. In 1846 William Cullen Bryant predicted the Island's future as a tourist spot "filled with cottages and boarding houses."

In an 1870 letter Dr. R.H. Mills wrote, "no better place can be found for chlerotic (*sic*) girls and puny boys," touting the benefits of Mackinac Island's healthful air and climate. In 1873, Island-born Thomas Ferry, U.S. Senator from Michigan, introduced a resolution into Congress to preserve federal land on Mackinac Island. In 1875 a national park was created on the Island which prohibited "settlement" of all the federal land. It was our nation's second national park, established only two years after Yellowstone.

The early nineteenth century tourists came for the challenge of Mackinac, but after the Civil War, people came to have fun. Tourism exploded in the 1880s. In 1881 the railroad came to Mackinaw City, and recognizing an opportunity, the Arnold Line began regular ferry service bringing tourists to the Island literally by the boatload. In 1882 Gurdon Hubbard began offering lots in "Hubbard's Annex" for wealthy Chicagoans to build summer cottages. Cottage construction on the East and West Bluffs began in 1885. In the spring of 1887 Plank's Grand Hotel was built in just 4 months. All of those tourists needed a big porch.

While it had been little more than a boarding house for military reserves for more than 50 years, by 1890 it became clear that Fort Mackinac had completely lost any military significance. The War Department abandoned the fort for the last time in 1894, and favored selling the federal lands protected in the National Park. In an effort that marked the beginning of political agility on Mackinac Island, citizens acted quickly to lobby Congress and identify a sympathetic senator, James McMillan. With the help of McMillan, by March of 1895, a bill was passed authorizing the Secretary of War to turn over the National Park to the State of Michigan. That same year Michigan made Mackinac Island its first State Park, beginning the current era of tourism.

The steam boat *Walk-in-the-Water* stopped at Mackinac Island in 1819. Although this wasn't a scheduled ferry, it marked the beginning of mass transit to Mackinac Island. It was the first of the steamers to negotiate Mackinac's harbor. One of Mackinac's most notable visitors, William Beaumont, arrived *On the Voyage*. Ships continued to leave passengers at Mackinac throughout the nineteenth century and tourism began to grow. When the railroad came to Mackinaw City in 1881, Arnold Transit began regular ferry service and an industry was born.

Today, nearly everyone who visits Mackinac Island arrives via one of three ferry services. In peak season the three services—Arnold, Sheppler and Star Line—run more than 100 trips a day to and from the Island. The ferries are the island's great equalizers. Even the wealthiest seasonal residents, who might often arrive at the airport, need to take ferries to get to their cars in Mackinaw City or St. Ignace. School kids from Gladwin on a field trip to Fort Mackinac ride on the same ferry with bigwig politicians heading for a conference at Grand Hotel. (Although politicians are prone to select the Arnold or Sheppler lines depending on their party affiliation, it is not exactly clear if independents must ride the Star Line.) There is perhaps no more complex human alloy, both culturally and financially, than the group coming down the gangplank at Mackinac Island.

Of course, to the knowledgeable, distinctions can be easily made and Island wanna-bes are wise to observe a few key points on ferry-riding savvy. A rider's level of sophistication can

be determined even before he or she boards a boat. Commuters know the ferry schedules as they know their own telephone numbers, and they will not waste time waiting on the dock. Hence, anyone queuing up before the boat arrives can be identified as a beginner. Standing in the loading area more than five minutes before boarding, even if the boat has arrived, is a dead giveaway that the rider is a tourist.

Carefully timed arrival at the dock is also important when leaving the Island. Commuters, Islanders headed to the grocery store, and Park Commission employees on their way to a meeting will use every second. They will linger in conversations with friends along Market Street, or chat with Mandy at Martha's. You will not see them glance at their watches, but at the last second they will stop the conversation with, "I've got to get a boat," and be gone. They arrive at the dock only after the luggage is loaded and the tourists have all headed for the seats on the top deck. There is no prize for being the last one to board, but few commuters can resist a self-serving smile when they walk up the gangplank just as the deck hands are lifting it from the dock.

On the boat, the decorum is really quite simple. Top decks, and the front of the boat on any deck are strictly off-limits to the frequent floater. Seasoned riders will often stand at back of the boat rather than take an empty window seat in the front of the boat. All commuters are allowed one exception to this rule and may climb to the top deck on any day in May when the wind is calm and the temperature is above 75°. Even then, they should avoid gazing at the bridge at all costs.

Even departing the boat can be done with style. Never crowd into the back of the boat. Don't wait at the stern for your bike. Finally, never ask about your luggage. If you have checked it on the mainland, it will likely get to your hotel. Certainly mistakes are made, but it's a small island, and most bags find their owners before sundown. More importantly, inquiring after your luggage will do little to assure its safe arrival.

Don't be shy about surveying the dock as if you are expecting someone to meet you. While it seems counterintuitive, both waiting for friends on the dock, and having friends waiting for you on the dock, are encouraged. Mackinac Island is, after all, about enjoyment and friendship. Islanders who wait on the docks for their friends and family are recognized as showing the highest level of hospitality. Even top-deck sitting tourists are seen as lucky by Islanders when they are observed in a warm embrace amid the chaos of Mackinac Island's ferry docks.

On Mackinac Island, everyone wants *To Be an Insider*, but few truly are. There is a carefully established pecking order of coolness on Mackinac Island, and who is at the top changes depending on where you fit. To add to the confusion, your personal status may change from season to season, or even from day to day.

The bottom is pretty well established: the Fudgie. But this dubious designation is carefully defined by some. A 1989 book, *Mackinac Connection*, defines a Fudgie as "The name given to day tourists by islanders" (interestingly, the book doesn't give a definition for "islanders," but more on that later). No one wants to overtly disparage The Tourist, particularly not visitors who spend a few nights on the Island and eat a half a dozen or so meals downtown, the people who might well be called the "blue chips" of Mackinac Island. Still, in the past, the term "Fudgie" might have been loosely applied to anyone who spends less time on Mackinac Island than you do. True insiders, however, realize that using the name "Fudgie" has lost its style, and is a sign that the speaker is close to being what the term itself describes. Still, most agree that those who walk down the gangplank at 11:00 a.m. and head back to Mackinaw City for dinner at Burger King on the 5:00 p.m. boat are dilettantes.

The next tier is firmly held by the seasonal employees who live on the Island in housing that makes college dorms look plush. They make fudge and bus tables. They drive teams of

LEFT: *From the Fort Holmes Hill, the panoramic view to the east doesn't include even one building.*

horses and speed down Main Street with suitcase-loaded handlebars. Seasonal employees are the muscle of Mackinac Island. They pay dearly for living on the Island by accepting lower wages that wouldn't lure the next group—the commuters—onto the boat. But there are perks. Few miss the free meal offered to them at St. Anne's on Friday evenings or the folksy square dancing on Tuesdays. Seasonal employees have been known to drink, and the Island itself is

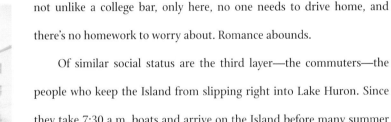

not unlike a college bar, only here, no one needs to drive home, and there's no homework to worry about. Romance abounds.

Of similar social status are the third layer—the commuters—the people who keep the Island from slipping right into Lake Huron. Since they take 7:30 a.m. boats and arrive on the Island before many summer residents peek out, everyone thinks they live on the Island. They are electricians, carpenters, plumbers, and gardeners. Their coolers are for lunch, not bottled water. They fall asleep on the 7:00 p.m. boat, not to feign indifference (as might a seasonal resident), but because they are exhausted from trying to earn an annual income in just three months.

The social hierarchy of the next three levels is subjective, the occupants of each category—summer residents, seasonal residents, and Islanders—each considering themselves at the top.

Whether they are wearing them or not, laboring commuters are sometimes called "Carhartts" for their work clothes. It isn't exactly complimentary.

Summer residents don't rush to get to the Island in the spring. They might not even make it for Lilac Festival. Many of them spend less time on the Island than most commuters, but they are established in the pecking order because they own land, or at least lease the land under the really big houses they own. They spend money on Mackinac Island—lots of it. The summer residents consider the next tier—seasonal residents—only slightly below them; they will allow their children to date each other. The summer residents might also observe that some of the seasonal residents work hard to keep up the appearance that they are not on the Island to earn a living.

Seasonal residents are the dairy farmers of Mackinac Island, milking the cash cows—some of them enjoying the cream. They own cottages, condos, entire blocks. Or they pay rents that would make a New Yorker flinch. They get to the Island in spring and usually see a leaf or two change color. Their greatest challenge is securing a solid supply of seasonal employees and commuters. They are characterized by a propensity to take a two week vacation away from Mackinac Island in July, usually to Europe. They often confuse themselves with summer residents, maintaining lovely porches and splendid cottages that sit empty most

*Regardless of pecking order, teenaged girls enjoy a charmed life on Mackinac Island. Transportation is
readily available and in the seemingly safe Mackinac environment, parents often relax a normally vigilant eye.
Finally, the shortage of babysitters is so profound that a responsible 14-year-old is like solid gold.*

of the day while they are at work. They have a hard time telling the difference between a commuter and an Islander.

The Islanders own the place. At the same time, there's no line at the dock to join the Islander crowd. In fact, with a census of about 700, there are fewer Islanders now than there were in the middle of the nineteenth century. They tolerate the influx of everyone else because they know they'll eventually leave. Islanders hold their heads high for having the fortitude to make it through the winter without completely losing their minds. The criteria for Islander status are simple: Their children go to school on the Island; they don't have a forwarding address; and their snowmobiles are newer than their cars. Summer residents and seasonal residents, specifically those of the third or fourth generation—who call themselves "Old Mackinac People"—would rather die than be considered Islanders.

Most enviable of all Mackinac Island denizens are the tourists, and they don't even know it. They stay for a few days, just long enough to enjoy an evening stroll on the boardwalk, and if they're lucky, a sunset and a round of golf at Wawashkamo. They don't stay long enough to realize that for three days their diet has been nearly void of produce. The cannon blasts and musket fire from the fort still quaintly punctuate the passing of their day. They hardly notice

Where do your kids go to school? Islanders can be best defined as people whose children are still enrolled at the Mackinac Island Public School after the first of November. The student body of under one hundred students can shrink by as much as one-third in the off-season.

the layer of dried manure dust on their shoes and bicycles. As they sit for a few hours on the porch reading a book, they can image what a delight it must be to live on Mackinac, without ever knowing how hard it is to fix a drain in the crawl space of a 100 year-old cottage because there are no plumbers on the Island. Tourists have the good life. Mackinac Island, with all of its charms and illusions, is here for them to enjoy.

Certain men find themselves bored on Mackinac Island. The whole Victorian thing is lost on them, and strolling through shops downtown is nothing short of punishment. For those men, *The Only Remedy Is Golf*. Grand Hotel offers 18 holes on the only course in the country where golfers get to the back nine via horse and carriage. The modestly challenging course offers some striking views of the Straits and a cross wind on the 9th fairway reminiscent of Pebble Beach. Still, to the adventurous golfer, the real charm of Mackinac, and a once-in-a-lifetime experience, lies just north of the airport at a private club that is open to the public.

Golf debuted on Mackinac Island in 1896 when a rough course was built on Mackinac Island near Grand Hotel. At the same time, four Chicago physicians, who all had cottages in Hubbard's Annex, laid out their own six-hole course in a pasture. The cows ended up winning that battle, but in 1898 the physicians' rough course led to the establishment of Wawashkamo Golf Course across the Island on Michael Dousman's farm. By 1900 the members had built the Wawashkamo clubhouse, setting the future of golf on Mackinac Island.

Scotsman Alex Smith designed the original Wawashkamo, giving it a true links pedigree. In the early part of the twentieth century the course was redesigned, its holes lengthened to reflect the sophistication of both players and their equipment, but some of the original features remain. Today golfers get the unique experience of shooting around gumdrops—three mounds of earth—and over a circus ring, an 18-inch-tall lump of grass that encircles the 3rd green.

LEFT AND ABOVE: *The front nine of Grand Hotel's Jewel golf course. The fenceline along the 8th fairway marks the boundary of the eighteenth century village, where there was once a stockade wall.*

For more than a century, as trends in golf have come and gone, "Wawa" has stayed true to its Scottish heritage, sometimes with great risk.

The 1960s were hard times for rustic golf courses. New color televisions brought weekly pictures of perfectly groomed courses over sweeping landscapes. The funky, rustic Wawashkamo was no match for these lush beauties. By January of 1964 Wawashkamo was nearly broke and had only 9 members. A proposal was made to have the Mackinac Island State Park Commission assume responsibility for the course and was even approved. The club's autonomy was saved, however, when the near-fatal heart attack of the club president tabled the proposal just long enough for two younger club members to stop the take-over.

Since its near demise in the 1960s, Wawashkamo has enjoyed a renewed interest in its historical significance. Throughout the 1970s, when other private clubs were being forced to open their doors to women, it was noted that Wawashkamo Golf club was open to them from its very beginning, even before they had the right to vote. Other clubs had allowed women to play if their husbands were members, but the Wawashkamo membership has long included women without regard to their family status. In 1996 Golf Digest named Wawashkamo one of America's Historic Golf Landmarks. It was the only nine-hole course in the dozen they listed. Perhaps most historically important is what is under the course.

In 1982 Wawashkamo was named a Michigan State Historic Site. The bloodiest battle

ever fought on Mackinac Island began and ended on August 4, 1814. American soldiers who were killed that day are probably buried under Wawashkamo Golf Course, the site of the battle. After the battle, the victorious British Commander, Robert McDouall assured that every casualty was buried on the site. There are suggestions that the remains were moved at the beginning of the twentieth century, but in 1999 historian Phil Porter wrote: "There is no record

The circus ring at Wawashkamo.

of these bodies being disinterred and they most likely remain on the old battlefield." In their book, *Walk a Crooked Trail*, Straus and Dunnigan suggest the bodies from the 1814 battle are buried under "a rough between Wawashkamo's 5th and 6th fairways."

Historically important both in terms of golf and American history, Wawashkamo remains one of the few respites on the Island. On all but the busiest days, a golfer can secure a tee time pretty much just by showing up. Even on a busy Fourth of July weekend, when tourists jam downtown and a bike ride around the Island can feel a bit like the Grand Prix, a round at Wawashkamo will test your swing, not your patience.

ABOVE: *The Wawashkamo Clubhouse.*

RIGHT: *The view from Wawashkamo's 15th tee.*

Patrick Sinclair liked the look of Mackinac Island. When he floated by in 1779, he saw the lime-stone bluff *Towering Over the Straits* of Mackinac. He knew that he would have a commanding view from the top of that hill. His hunch was correct: there are no more dramatic Island views than those from Fort Mackinac. As it happens, Sinclair was thinking about the strategic value of the bluff, and history has shown that he underestimated the fort's vulnerability from the north. In fact, the fort had only brief military significance, and failed when it was tested. More than 200 years later, however, Sinclair's great contribution to Mackinac Island's glory is clear. He built a military outpost perfectly suited to becoming a tourism landmark.

Built by the British in the 1780s, Fort Mackinac saw its first conflict under the American flag during the War of 1812. In July of 1812 Lieutenant Porter Hanks, the fort's commander, was not concerned about the threat of war, and only learned that war had been declared when he heard the warning shot fired from the British cannon on the bluff that is now called Fort Holmes. Fort Mackinac's first test was over in one shot. Hanks surrendered.

In July of 1814 the Americans tried to retake the Island with an attack from the north shore, as had the British in 1812. The British knew they were coming, however, and met the Americans in the center of the Island. It was the most significant battle ever fought on

As it did in the eighteenth century, Fort Mackinac dominates the high ground in Mackinac's harbor.

Mackinac Island. Although the Americans suffered only 20 casualties, they lost the battle. Their success on the battlefield notwithstanding, the British were not destined to hold the fort; it was returned to the Americans six months later in a treaty settlement.

Between 1812 and 1814, while they held the Island, the British built Fort George on the hill above Fort Mackinac. Later, the Americans renamed it Fort Holmes. Revealing the military insignificance of troops on Mackinac Island, Fort Holmes, clearly a better strategic position, was abandoned in favor of the indefensible but more cosmopolitan and convenient Fort Mackinac. The 1814 battle marks the last time there was military tension at Fort Mackinac.

After American troops retook the fort in 1815, it became a holding area for U.S. forces. Since there was nothing to protect, the fort was abandoned whenever its troops were needed to fight battles in the South and West. The relative safety of life at the fort is told in the morbidity records of the soldiers stationed there. A list of the soldiers buried at the post cemetery reveals that disease and accidents were the greatest risks faced by Fort Mackinac soldiers. Among the tragedies was Andrew O. Simonson, who died on July 4, 1870 when he was killed while firing the traditional holiday cannon salute.

A tour of duty at the fort became even safer in 1875 when more than 900 acres outside the fort and 10 acres inside the fort were designated Mackinac Island National Park, the second

A concert of military music is performed daily in high season, but throughout the day reenactors practice period tunes. When the bagpipes, fife, and drum echo between the fort's buildings and mix with the clomping of horses downtown, even the most cynical will feel that they have stepped into the nineteenth century.

national park in the United States. The fort became the national park's administrative head-
quarters. In the 1880s Fort Mackinac was a plum assignment for military personnel. Harold
Dunbar Corbusier's diary reveals the low level of risk that the soldiers faced. Corbusier, an
eleven-year-old boy whose father was stationed at Fort Mackinac in 1883 and 1884, was
primarily concerned about skating conditions, a pastime only briefly interrupted when his
mother and brother fell ill. In fact the greatest threats to those serving at the fort were drown-
ing and illnesses related to exposure.

Twenty-first century visitors to Fort Mackinac will see displays and costumes that recreate the 1880s. It may be that the sort of leisurely reenacting of military life that tourists see in the fort today exactly mirrors the risk-free life of Victorian Fort Mackinac. A photograph from 1882 shows wives and children of soldiers, sitting on the hill near the north block house watching soldiers drill on the parade ground, exactly as visitors watch interpreters today.

In 1895 Mackinac Island, and with it the fort, became Michigan's first State Park. The historical and cultural value wasn't immediately apparent to those charged with the management of the park. There was little funding from the state, and after museum displays in the Officers' Stone Quarters were proposed, it took nearly twenty years to get them installed. Fort Mackinac was in need of repair, and it would be decades before it was recognized as the historical center of Mackinac Island. The fort might have been more significantly altered, but for a lack of money and manpower Fort Mackinac was mostly used as it was, leaving its basic structure unchanged since it was built in the 1780s.

Through the first half of the twentieth century the Fort buildings were used as administrative offices and for staff housing with limited exhibits. Visitors climbed the hill to wander the mostly empty fort. People had picnics on the gun platforms. In the 1950s the children of Governor G. Mennen Williams, as well as other Island kids, were known to play daily on the parade ground.

The one-time lack of respect for history is illustrated by the switching of grave markers at the Post Cemetery. In 1906 or 1907, Park Superintendent B. F. Emery removed the wooden markers and replaced them with stones, to "even it up and make it look better." In some cases graves were mismarked and remain incorrect today.

Today's Fort Mackinac, with museum displays and professional interpreters, can be traced back to the late 1950s when Grand Hotel owner W. Stewart Woodfill led the Park Commission in getting revenue bonds approved for the restoration of the fort. A fee of 50¢ for

In 1999 the wall under the Lower Gun Platform crumbled during the night. It wasn't the first time. Americans were concerned about the wall when they took control of the fort in 1796. A 1903 commission report noted, "the fort wall shows signs of weakening." Shortly after that report, the wall gave way in roughly the same area. Although it's a difficult task, maintaining the wall is a high priority. The fort wall is believed to be one of the oldest structures in Michigan.

adults and 25¢ for children was established amid a brief storm of controversy. The winds of available revenue soon dispersed the quarrelling, and an era of restoration began.

Today Fort Mackinac is something of an open-air museum. Women in Victorian costume play games with children on the parade ground. The hourly cannon and rifle firing demonstrations mark time all the way to Grand Hotel. But a significant part of the experience is still the unrestricted views available from along the stockade wall and fort buildings. From the West Blockhouse you can look across Grand Hotel's golf course to the bridge. It's the same view that allowed fort commanders to keep an eye on activity in the nineteenth century "shanty town," an encampment of fishermen in the area between Grand Hotel and the Island school. From the Officers' Stone Quarters or the porch of the Post Canteen, you can see every boat coming in and out of the harbor. You look down on the town that Patrick Sinclair established below the fort more than 200 years ago. The North Blockhouse offers you a view to the bluff above Fort Mackinac, from where Lieutenant Hanks and his troops took cannon fire that July day in 1812.

When the summer sun takes temperatures into the 90s, there is always a breeze on the Upper Gun Platform. Whenever ferry boats come into the harbor, if children are playing a game of tag in Marquette Park, for as long as Lakes Michigan and Huron are blue, Fort Mackinac will be the best seat in the house.

A Chronology of Fort Mackinac

OCTOBER 1779 .... British commander Patrick Sinclair checks out Mackinac Island on his way to Michilimackinac. He likes the bluffs and cuts a deal with the natives. Construction begins almost at once.

MAY 12, 1781 .... Ojibway chiefs sign a deed giving the Island to the British. They get 12 canoes loaded with trade goods worth £5,000.

MAY 1783 .... Paris Peace Treaty puts Mackinac Island in the U.S.; British Captain Robertson stops all work on the fort, but he and his troops stay.

SEPTEMBER 1, 1796 .... Under Jay's Treaty the Americans take command of the fort. It is falling apart.

JULY 17, 1812 .... Before he even gets word that war has been declared, Lt. Porter Hanks surrenders after one warning shot from the north. British retake the fort.

DECEMBER 24, 1814 .... The Treaty of Ghent restores all lands captured by the British to the Americans, including Fort Mackinac.

JULY 18, 1815 .... U.S. Forces retake command of the fort.

1837 .... U.S. Soldiers are sent from Fort Mackinac to Florida for the 2nd Seminole War.

1840 .... Troops return.

1848 .... Fort is abandoned for one year. Soldiers sent to the Mexican War. Caretaker Sergeant William Marshall remains.

1857-58 .... Fort is abandoned. Soldiers are sent to the Santee Indian Uprising. Caretaker Sergeant William Marshall remains.

1861	Fort is abandoned. Soldiers are sent to the Civil War. Sergeant William Marshall remains.
1862	"Stanton Guard" established at Fort Mackinac to guard three Confederate political prisoners. When the prisoners are released the fort is again abandoned.
SUMMER 1865 & 1866	Veteran Reserve Corps occupy the fort.
AUGUST 1867	Troops return to the fort.
1875	National Park established. Fort officers become park superintendents.
1876	Additional soldiers sent to help administer the National Park.
1881	Hot and cold running water are installed. Soldiers are required to bathe at least weekly.
OCTOBER 9, 1894	Majority of troops are withdrawn, fort abandoned.
SEPTEMBER 16, 1895	Fort Mackinac becomes part of Michigan's first State Park.
1896	Mackinac Island State Park Commission proposes using the Officers' Stone Quarters as a museum.
1915	Museum displays are installed in the Officers' Stone Quarters.
1933	Temporary 10¢ fee charged for admission.
1958	Revenue bonds are issued for restoration. Fees of 50¢ for adults and 25¢ for children are established, and the days of free entry to the fort end forever.

From the middle of June through Labor Day *An Army of Teenagers* marches through the streets of Mackinac. They are the Boy Scouts and Girls Scouts who bring a rare enthusiasm to their daily rituals, preserving the traditions of Mackinac Island.

Each morning at 9:00 the first group marches in formation down Huron Road and turns left at Fort Street. They march down the hill past the Governor's residence and into town to take their positions at flagpoles throughout the village. Ten minutes later a second unit marches through the fort, some stopping at the avenue of flags and others at the big flag pole near the Hill Quarters. The last few march down the ramp overlooking Marquette Park to take their positions two by two at each flag pole along the hill. One scout blows reveille from the porch of the Post Canteen, and with mechanical precision the flags are raised all over Mackinac Island. The day begins.

The Mackinac Island Scout Service Camp is host to one troop each week of the summer. The scouts live in the barracks across Huron Road from the fort. They eat and bunk together. They march, play, and explore together. They have campfires in Greany Grove and take evening ferry cruises around the Island. At the end of a week they have joined a group of more than 30,000 scouts who have served at Fort Mackinac.

The program started in 1929, when eight Eagle Scouts were asked to help out at the fort for one month. Gerald R. Ford, then a teenager, was among them. When Ford returned for a

visit in 1975 as President of the United States, his helicopter landed under the cover of darkness in the open area in front of the scout barracks.

From the 1930s through the 1940s the scouts served as tour guides in the fort, until costumed guides were hired by the Park Commission in the 1950s. Girl Scouts served for the first time in 1974 when troops from Ann Arbor and Grosse Pointe Farms each served one week. Although there has never been a quota, today the camp is staffed half of the summer by Girl Scout troops. The scouts help as guides at the Biddle House, McGulpin House, Beaumont Memorial and Indian Dormitory as well as Fort Mackinac. They greet visitors and direct them on the tour of the Governor's residence. They bring a respect to the daily raising and lowering the flags that is rarely found outside of military ceremonies. On an island where commercialism often rules the day, the scouts are a wholesome reminder of everything right about Mackinac.

At the end of each week the scouts march in formation to the ferry docks, changed for their experience, while a new troop marches off the ferry, through town and up Fort Street into Mackinac Island history.

OPPOSITE: *In addition to raising and lowering the flag, each scout troop decides which flag to fly from the main flagpole near the Hill Quarters. When the wind is light, Troop #1 from Port Huron chooses the Big Flag. Folding the 70-pound flag is a ballet that requires nearly the entire troop.*

One warm July afternoon Lorabeth Fitzgerald looked out the window of her East Bluff cottage.
"Have You Been to the Soldiers' Garden?" she asked. She was talking about Mackinac roads less traveled, about places of reverence. People on Mackinac develop personal connections. The ties are not obvious, not what you might think.

The Soldiers' Garden is a clearing on the north east side of the Island. It's as close to nowhere as you can get on an island that's only eight miles around. Over time the brush has encroached, leaving only a small circle of grasses and wildflowers that glow with color in the spring. There isn't room for an infield. You couldn't play volleyball there, even if you had a net. Certainly hikers have walked through it without knowing they were Somewhere.

It isn't even clear that soldiers ever used the Soldiers' Garden. In the nineteenth century, the fort gardens were maintained in the area that is now Marquette Park. It may have been used as a grain field, but it seems unlikely since the clearing is so far from either fort.

The Soldiers' Garden itself isn't marked; trails from both Leslie Avenue and Crooked Tree Road are identified with small signs reading "Soldiers' Garden Trail." Even the signs, hidden in the brush, are easy to miss. For as hard as it is to find, the Soldiers' Garden doesn't offer a dramatic reward. It's a nice place to read a book, a good place for a nap or a rest after the long hike from town. It isn't for everyone.

Despite its natural features, Mackinac Island is defined by three dozen summer retreats.

Like Jewels on a Crown, the cottages sparkle from the East and West Bluffs framing the Island. Although there are less than 40 cottages on the two bluffs, and less than

100 when Hubbard's Annex and the cottages in town are included, people associate Mackinac Island with cottage life. Perhaps it's because multi-sided towers and wrap-around porches face public streets, or because the ornaments on the Gothic cottages are visible from the decks of every incoming ferry. Either way, Mackinac Island is noted for its Victorian charm, a setting created by a few summer homes built over 100 years ago.

Both economic and cultural forces were in action to begin the great cottage boom of the late nineteenth century, but when Gurdon Hubbard built "The Lilacs" in 1870, he got the ball rolling. Then in 1875 when Mackinac Island became a national park, included in the law was a provision to allow leases for summer cottages. Almost immediately there were requests to build cottages on the federal land, but for bureaucratic problems, such as a lack of an accurate survey, the leases were not approved for nearly

There is great debate regarding the views from East and West Bluffs, with the occupants of each preferring theirs. While the view debate is without resolution, as one long-timer put it, "the general consensus is that the West Bluff has the money, but the East Bluff has the brains." In both cases—wealth and intelligence—the comparison is relative.

LEFT: *East bluff porches look south to Lake Huron.*

ABOVE: *Mackinac's signature view of the turrets of the West Bluff.*

ten years. In the meantime, Hubbard platted "Hubbard's Annex" on his 80 acres, and began offering lots for sale in 1882, the same year the Detroit and Cleveland Steam Navigation Company began regular service to Mackinac Island. He sold his first lot in 1883, and during the spring and summer of that year eight annex cottages were constructed.

The first cottages on leased land were built on East Bluff in 1885. In 1886 construction began on the West Bluff. Grand Hotel was built in just four months in 1887 and the era of Victorian life on Mackinac Island began. By 1895 there were more than 30 cottages on the two bluffs, nearly the total today.

In 1895, Michigan's Mackinac Island State Park Commission took over the national park, and the first controversy over lease rates erupted. In an effort to raise money for the management of Michigan's new state park, the MISPC doubled the rates on leased lots from $50 to $100 per year. Time smoothed over any rough edges created between the Commission and the lease holders, but it wasn't the last time there was turmoil over the land under Mackinac Island's most desirable addresses.

In 1933, at the peak of the Great Depression, the Park Commission was doing anything it could to keep the cottages occupied. They discounted lease rates for anyone making timely payments and cut them again if the cottages were occupied. Still cottages went into foreclosure

Because they are on private land, cottages in Hubbard's Annex are more secluded than most other historic cottages.

and by the end of the 1930s, the commission owned several East and West Bluff cottages. They offered them for sale, ranging in price from $300 to $2,000 and still some of them didn't sell for years. It was 1946 before all the cottages were back in private hands, and the last cottage was purchased for $1,000 with only $250 cash down.

Going into the 1950s, Commissioners were satisfied just to see all of the cottages being properly maintained under private ownerships. Soon, they required fort admission fees to

As the cottages become more valuable, some owners are tempted to redecorate to a
higher level of sophistication, but it's still simple cottage style that best suits Mackinac.

generate income. As a result, lease fees were ignored until the late part of the century when they became a seemingly valuable political tool. In 1991, the story broke that lease rates on cottages hadn't changed since the Depression. Cottages worth half a million dollars were sitting on lots that leased for $100 a year. The disparity was part tradition and part oversight, but was

used in an attempt to embarrass the newly elected governor and the Park Commission he appointed. The newspaper report attempted to paint Island cottage owners as the greedy rich. The image didn't take. There was local complaining when the Park Commission raised lease rates with subsequent annual increases based on inflation, but the whole incident had no long-term political consequences, and only served to bring the Island some undeserved negative attention. In the end, cottagers paid the rents and the whole controversy quickly disappeared. No one gives up a treasured family cottage for a lease increase that amounts to about a week's stay at Grand Hotel.

Mackinac Island and its original Victorian cottages cannot be separated. In the 1990s a major home fashions designer introduced a line of wallpaper and fabrics based on Mackinac's cottage trends. National magazines visit regularly for features on Victorian life. Where land is available development continues today. Million-dollar homes that take more than a season to build are designed to match the architecture of nineteenth century cottages that were built in two months for $3,000. Third-generation cottage owners still cherish every moment they spend on the porch, rocking back and forth into more than a century of tradition that has defined Mackinac Island.

*All that glitters is not Victorian. On Mackinac Island when the sun is low in the west
and pours through windows like gold, any place to call your own is a great comfort.*

ABOVE AND LEFT: *In 1901 Lawrence A. Young of Chicago was granted a lease for a cottage on the bluff just west of the fort. At that time, the village pasture was just below, where the front nine of the Grand Hotel golf course is today. It was among the cottages that fell into poor repair during the Great Depression, and was purchased in 1945 by the Mackinac Island State Park Commission to curry favor with the Governor of Michigan. Because of its position alone on the bluff, the Governor's residence looks appropriately regal. In fact, it's not among the largest cottages on the Island, and is maintained as a simple but elegant summer retreat. Perhaps the greatest perk enjoyed by the governor's family is the best view on the Island.*

Mackinac Island rides on the backs of hundreds of horses. Horses pulled the scraper that cut the shore road. They haul cargo and entertain tourists. Most importantly, they give Mackinac Island a character that is unique in the civilized world. There are other glamourous islands. Martha's Vineyard shimmers in the Atlantic, but the army of black Mercedes rolling through its small towns, and its swarm of buzzing mopeds give it the hustle of nearby Boston. Michigan's Beaver Island is quiet and remote, but its proliferation of old tractors and rusty Toyotas make it feel mostly like a forgotten farm town. Mackinac Island alone is a respite from motorized transportation, and we owe it all to huge four-legged creatures with names like Lucky and Otis, Woody and Duce.

The Cadence of Hoof Beats is the official rhythm of Mackinac Island. Children stand in awe. Tourists fumble for their cameras to snap the polished Grand Hotel carriages, their drivers in red coats and top hats. Horses rule Mackinac Island. Bicycles are expected to give them right of way. No one makes a fuss when horses relieve themselves while dignitaries disembark at the Governor's residence. The teamsters admonish visitors standing in the road with a firm, "Watch the horses!" They rarely say "please."

The militia of horses requires a battalion of human commanders, most of whom work for Mackinac Island Carriage Tours, a company formed in 1948 from what was left of The Carriagemen's Coalition. The Coalition was founded in 1932 to create ethical standards for

ABOVE LEFT: *The familiar yellow-and-red carriages carry 200,000 tourists a year.*

ABOVE RIGHT: *One of Grand Hotel's vintage enclosed carriages.*
The Grand Stables are the only part of the hotel open to the public without a fee.

OPPOSITE: *Fetse is part of the team Jay Stingel drives four-in-hand.*
A few residents maintain their own teams, most of them beautiful animals lovingly kept.

carriage drivers, to stop the unscrupulous from working the docks for customers. It wasn't

uncommon for tourists to be aggressively solicited while they came down the ferry gangplanks.

It may be, however, that those pre-Coalition drivers were simply giving the tourists what they

wanted. Today, the Carriage Tours ticket office is directly across the street from the Arnold

Dock, and a steady flow of tourists can be observed moving directly from the dock onto one of

The end of each tourist season is marked by the procession of horses off the Island.
They are tied together in teams of four and led in groups of twenty or more horses
from the stables, down Turkey Hill Road, through town, and to the
docks. After the short boat ride they spend a relaxed winter near St. Ignace.

the trademark red-and-yellow tour carriages.

Teamsters are still the rough edges of Mackinac Island. It's difficult to put on airs when you spend your day at the exhaust end of a horse, and carriage drivers don't try. On an island filled with brightly painted cottages they wear dark brown or dark green uniforms. They bulk up in the Carriage Tours cafeteria, open only to employees, where all-you-can-eat meals are served three times a day. But tour customers like their candor, and Island residents rely on them for transportation and delivery. As long as there are destinations, there will be teamsters.

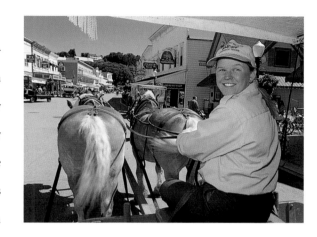

America, and most of the rest of the world, is addicted to movement. We need to get somewhere, and we need to get there soon. More importantly, we don't want to rely on our feet to make the trip for us. A two-mile walk is an exercise program, not a reasonable stroll to a dinner engagement. Without cars to get us across town, we need horses. Early on, the bureaucrats on Mackinac Island recognized the importance of horse power. The timing may be coincidental, but once the auto ban was enacted in 1900, the park commission established a license fee of $1 to $3 for each horse drawn carriage. It began a tradition of regulation and control that still continues. Today there are specific limits on the number of carriages, taxis, and drays

ABOVE LEFT: *It's not Oklahoma, but tour carriages and most taxis have fringe on top.*

ABOVE RIGHT: *Why is this woman smiling? Despite the dust, the pay is good, housing—with maid service—is provided, and as there are few with the skill required to drive a team, the job is secure.*

allowed on the Island. Even the route tour carriages may take, where they will stop, and what their drivers will wear are dictated by agreements with the Park Commission. In addition to keeping the horse traffic manageable, in some ways, the limits provide the unintended benefit of reducing the rush of development.

The key to preservation on Mackinac Island hasn't been conservancy programs that protect land. It wasn't zoning ordinances. It was transportation, or the lack of it. It's hard to quickly build a 4,000-square-foot home when every stick needs to be carried to the site on a flat-bed horse cart. The more remote the location, the more difficult the logistics. Although the current law forbids the Commission from "Permitting the use of motor vehicles," the greatest challenge of the twenty-first century will be controlling the erosion of the auto ban that has crept into off-season Mackinac Island. The Labor Day bridge walk is barely over when the red, city pick-up truck starts to zip across town. No sooner do the Commissioners leave for Lansing in October than the green MISPC truck can be seen making runs down fort hill at lunch time. In the fall and spring, drive-yourself carriages compete with construction vehicles on M-185. Although Fort Mackinac, Grand Hotel, The Island House and many others were built without motorized vehicles, in recent years every construction project begins with special use permits to burn gasoline rather than carbohydrates. It's a trend that needs to be reversed.

LEFT: *When you have four feet, you need a lot of shoes. Island horses wear high-tech shoes made of polyurethane with steel inserts invented on Mackinac by "Dr. Bill" Chambers. He has also developed special feeds for the horses matched to the work load and season. It's no surprise that advances in horse technology would come from the Island, which supports the world's largest working livery.*

As it always has, horsepower will pull Mackinac into the next century. Kids learn about animals riding atop rental horses that guide them knowingly around the Island. Huge draft horses pull everything from trash to Fed-Ex packages. Everything gets there, but in its own sweet time. The Island's horses keep the pace. It's a slow steady rhythm that keeps Mackinac from moving too quickly into the future.

Fort Holmes is a favorite destination for rental horses.
The Henry Trail, now mostly used by rental horse riders on their way to
Fort Holmes, was once a carriage tour shortcut, nicknamed Suicide Hill.

The Photographs

RIGHT: *The Marquette statue was dedicated on September 1, 1909. Although Marquette was only 39 when he died, the portly 50ish looking figure depicted in the statue was the sculptor's interpretation, probably designed to make him look like then contemporary political leaders.*

OPPOSITE PAGE: *Lilacs have become the Island's signature planting. It is widely reported*
that the French Jesuits brought lilacs to Mackinac Island, but the story may not be true.
Long-time Grand Hotel owner and Mackinac Island visionary W. Stewart Woodfill
once said of the story, "There is absolutely no basis for it, as I invented it."

Devil's Kitchen.

ABOVE: *Trillium along the Juniper Trail. Because there are no deer grazing
on the island, its forest floors wear thick carpets of wildflowers.*

Harbor View Inn, view to St. Anne's Church.

The Iroquois Hotel.

Trinity church, at the base of Fort Hill watches over Marquette Park. Mackinac Island has been the center of spirituality for as long as history can recount. Perhaps it is the isolation from the sins of the mainland, things like cars and fast food. Maybe it's just that people have more time for God when they are on vacation. While we refer to the native teachings as "legend," there is something sacred about the Island

RIGHT: *A meadow just south of Leslie Avenue. Leslie Avenue was built in 1889 as a scenic drive and it still remains one of the most remote areas of the Island.*

They're not the same Anne.

LEFT: *Were it not for alert carriage drivers, more than a few visitors would have met their maker while standing in the middle of main street, their necks stretched up to ogle St. Anne's as it reaches to the clouds.*

ABOVE: *Anne's Tablet was named for a character in a book by Constance Fenimore Woolson set on Mackinac Island. The landmark is hidden at the west end of East Bluff. While the small alcove is secluded by brush, just beyond the trees, within earshot is the summer quarters for the director of the Mackinac Island State Park Commission. The juxtaposition more or less assures that Anne's Tablet is a quiet respite both day and night.*

The signature horse and carriage topiary at the top of Grand Hill.

RIGHT: *Even from the water, before the details are clear,*
the expanse of the Grand Hotel facade identifies Mackinac Island.

The protestant Mission Church was built in 1829. The mission ran a school until 1837
to bring religious civilization to the island. The school taught a curriculum of
basic skills to native children (trade skills to the boys and domestic skills to the girls)
while at the same time offering them salvation. Although the school lasted
only a few years, at its peak enrollment of 200 children it rivaled the head count
of Mackinac Island's current school which usually enrolls less than 100 students.

The Mackinac Bridge, the boardwalk and Grand Hotel viewed from the West Blockhouse.

West shore view to Round Island.

Brown's Brook is the island's only year-round stream.

In-line skates are not allowed in the Village of Mackinac Island. In the middle nineteenth century
when fishing was the Island's primary industry, there was a ban on the dumping of fish guts.
The modern in-line skate ban uses a similar boundary line.

*In early June riders on the North Bicycle Trail usually speed right by
dramatic clusters of yellow lady slippers. There are few places where these shy
orchids grow in such significant numbers, but only visitors who look between
the tall grass will enjoy their brief appearance.*

Mackinac Island is the Las Vegas of the north. Anyone on the island
for three consecutive days will encounter at least one wedding.

Sources

Andrews, Roger M. *Old Fort Mackinac on the Hill of History*. Menominee, MI. 1938.

Armour, David A., *100 years at Mackinac*. Mackinac State Historic Parks, Mackinac Island, MI. 1995.

Armour, David A., "Mackinac Island's Scout Service Camp," *Mackinac History,* Vol III. Mackinac State Historic Parks, Mackinac Island, MI. 1998

Gringhuis, Dirk. *The Lore of the Great Turtle: Indian Legends of Mackinac Retold*. State Historic Parks, Mackinac Island, MI. 1970.

Gringhuis, Dirk.*Were-Wolves and Will-O-the-Wisps: French Tales of Mackinac Retold*. State Historic Parks, Mackinac Island, MI. 1974.

Kelton, Dwight H. *Annals of Fort Mackinac*. Chicago. 1882. Reprinted, Mackinac State Historic Parks, Mackinac Island, MI. 1992.

McKee, Russell. *Mackinac: The Gathering Place*. Lansing, Michigan. 1981.

McVeigh, Amy. *Mackinac Connection: An Insider's Guide*. Mackinac Publishing. Mackinac Island, MI. 1989

Nicholas, Edward. *The Chaplain's Lady: Life and Love at Fort Mackinac*. Mackinac State Historic Parks, Mackinac Island, MI. 1987.

Petersen, Eugene T. *Inside Mackinac*. St. Ignace, Michigan, 1990

Petersen, Eugene T. *Mackinac Island, Its History in Pictures*. Mackinac State Historic Parks, Mackinac Island, MI. 1973

Porter, Phil, ed. *A Boy at Fort Mackinac: The Diary of Harold Dunbar Corbusier 1883-1884*, 1892. Mackinac State Historic Parks, Mackinac Island, MI. 1994

Porter, Phil, *Mackinac: An Ilsand Famous in These Regions*. Mackinac State Historic Parks, Mackinac Island, MI. 1998

Porter, Phil, "Mackinac Island's Post Cemetery," *Mackinac History, Vol III*. Mackinac State Historic Parks, Mackinac Island, MI. 1999

Porter, Phil, A *View from the Veranda*, Mackinac State Historic Parks, Mackinac Island, MI. 1981

Porter, Phil, *The Wonder of Mackinac*. Mackinac State Historic Parks, Mackinac Island, MI. 1984

Ranville, Judy, and Nancy Campbell. *Memories of Mackinaw*. Petoskey, Michigan. 1976.

Straus, Frank, and Brian Dunnigan, *Walk a Crooked Trail, A Centenial History of Wawashkamo Golf Club*, Mackinac Island, MI. 2000